MILLIONAIRE SECRETS

MILLIONAIRE SECRETS

JIM STEPHENS

Contents

1

Introduction to Wealth Building

Wealth is a concept that transcends mere financial gain; it encompasses a mindset, a strategy, and a lifestyle. The Bible references wealth over 2,000 times, with figures such as Solomon and Jesus having much to say about money and the principles of wealth building.

In today's society, individuals with varying degrees of wealth often face judgment for their material possessions and financial success. This perspective must shift for you to achieve the lifestyle you desire. The goal of this book is to instruct you on how to demand and achieve the luxuries of life that few can afford due to a lack of either ability or mindset. By accepting this challenge, you have already taken a significant step ahead of the majority. Your journey toward financial success and personal fulfillment has begun.

Understanding the Mindset of Millionaires

To think like a millionaire, one must adopt a mindset and psychology that differentiates the wealthy from the average individual. Self-made millionaires do not necessarily possess extraordinary skills, but they do have distinct behaviors and mental attitudes. The Whitney Group, boasting $600 million, exemplifies this mindset. Jeff Weber, a psychologist who has studied millionaires, emphasizes that the millionaire mindset is characterized by a high level of acceptance. They are inclined to say "yes" rather than "no," embracing opportunities and viewing the world differently.

This accepting mindset allows millionaires to see possibilities where others see obstacles. Whether making million-dollar deals or paying taxes, their openness to opportunities drives their success. This mindset is not bound by age or specific numbers; it is a universal trait among the wealthy, whether they are 18 or 72.

The phrase "I would rather be" is crucial for those aspiring to wealth. It reflects a desire to live life on one's terms, whether that means relaxing on a beach, retiring early, being debt-free, or working creatively. This powerful mindset encourages goal-setting and the pursuit of financial freedom. Writing down your goals can help foster this "I would rather be" thought process, leading to greater success and fulfillment.

2

Financial Foundations

In the quest for building and maintaining wealth, foundational financial strategies are essential. These strategies can be visualized as a pyramid, with the most basic practices forming the broad and sturdy base, supporting more advanced techniques at the top. The broader and more robust the base, the easier it is to build upward, ensuring long-term financial stability and growth.

At the heart of these foundational strategies is the simple yet powerful principle of **budgeting**: spend less than you earn. While straightforward in concept, achieving this requires a series of thoughtful decisions that collectively determine the soundness of your financial life. It's not just about spending less but also about **where** you allocate your funds, as this can significantly impact how quickly your money grows through compound interest and how it affects your lifestyle, liquidity, comfort, and even tax liability.

Our goal is to explore the various choices and practices that contribute to a solid financial foundation.

Budgeting and Saving Strategies

Budgeting is the cornerstone of wealth management. It begins with a clear understanding of your finances, which involves meticulously tracking your income and expenses to ensure every dollar is accounted for. Here are some strategies to help manage your expenses effectively:

1. **Track Your Income and Expenses:**
   - Record all the money you earn each month.
   - List all your expenses, including bills, car payments, and other recurring costs.
   - Calculate your disposable income (the money left after covering all expenses).
2. **Control Impulse Buying:**
   - Balance impulse purchases by setting short-term goals.
   - As you shop, focus on these goals to avoid unnecessary spending.
   - Develop the habit of watching every penny and plan for the long-term.

Saving is crucial, especially when you are young. It may seem challenging to put money aside when you feel like you have all the time in the world, but the sooner you start, the better. Here are some saving strategies:

1. **Pay Yourself First:**
   - Save a portion of your income before spending on anything else.
   - Aim to save at least 10% of your income.
2. **Maximize Your Savings:**
   - Even if you can't save 10%, save as much as you can.

- Consistently saving, such as $500 per month, allows you to accumulate wealth during your peak earning years (16-40 years old).
- Let compound interest work for you as your earnings potentially decrease after 40.

By the time you reach retirement, these habits will have helped you build a substantial nest egg. Remember, effective saving begins with prioritizing yourself—set aside savings before addressing other financial obligations.

3

Investment Strategies

Building wealth involves making your money work for you. While not everyone has the time or interest to engage in unique ventures like ticket scalping or entering shows to win prizes, there are numerous proven investment strategies that are less time-intensive and risky. Many self-made millionaires have utilized what can be termed the "Cents of Prosperity" strategies, where the choice of investments significantly influences net worth.

One of the most effective and popular ways to grow your wealth is through **investing in the stock market**.

Stock Market: Investing in the stock market is often considered the pinnacle method for earning a return on investment. Many millionaires have invested in the stock market due to its potential for high returns. Historically, a well-diversified portfolio of high-quality companies has returned an average of 11-12 percent annually. This rate of return, coupled with diligent investment, can lead to substantial wealth accumulation over time, potentially surpassing other income sources. It's important to note, however, that while the stock market has provided substantial returns historically, it comes with no guarantees for the future. Long-term profitability is key, and patience is essential to reap the benefits of above-average returns.

Stock Market Basics

The stock market is where you can buy and sell shares of ownership in companies, as well as other related securities such as stock options. Familiarize yourself with some essential elements and terminologies:

- **Bull Market:** A period when the market is on the rise, with more traders buying than selling.
- **Dividend:** A payment made by a company to its shareholders, usually derived from profits.
- **Initial Public Offering (IPO):** The first sale of stock by a private company to the public.
- **Stock Warrant:** A financial contract that gives the holder the right to purchase a company's stock at a specific price.
- **Stock Symbol:** The abbreviated trading symbol of a publicly traded company.
- **Volume:** The number of shares traded in a security or the entire market during a specific period.
- **Rally:** A sharp increase in stock prices.
- **Dividend Yield:** The annual dividend payment divided by the stock's current price, expressed as a percentage.

Before diving into the investment world, consider these basic questions:

1. **Why are you investing?**
2. **How much risk are you comfortable with?**
3. **What insider tips and basic strategies can guide your investments?**

Here are several key factors to consider when making investment decisions:

- **Research:** Conduct thorough research on the companies you plan to invest in.
- **Learn Trading Basics:** Understand trading methodologies and analytical tools.
- **Retirement Programs:** Contribute to employer-based retirement programs or other planned investments.
- **Solid Companies:** Focus on investing in solid companies and avoid the pitfalls of day trading.

By understanding these fundamental principles and strategies, you can make informed investment decisions that align with your financial goals.

4

Real Estate Investments

Property investment is a tried and true method for building wealth over the long term. It involves the ownership and rental of residential and/or commercial properties. Although it may not yield immediate returns, property investment can generate steady income over time, and property assets tend to appreciate significantly, offering substantial investment potential.

Management: Being a property owner often requires hands-on involvement, especially when something breaks or a property needs to be prepared for new tenants. Most property owners start as sole proprietors, reporting rental income as part of their total income. To maximize the value of a property, a manager must understand what drives an investment property's value. This includes knowledge of income and expense items and market and economic trends, which can help adjust rental prices and increase returns.

Leverage: Real estate is unique in its potential for leveraging. Investors can purchase multiple properties without full cash financing, increasing their portfolio size. Leveraging allows the use of borrowed funds to amplify potential returns. This strategy, often referred to as "pyramid power" by industry insiders, involves using other people's money to grow your investment portfolio. Historically, real estate ownership has proven to be one of the most stable and effective ways to grow wealth.

Investing in real estate, particularly residential properties, often requires a long-term horizon of 10-15 years. This approach allows new investors to build multi-property portfolios over 20-30 years, live comfortably, and potentially become seven-figure investors. The key lies in selecting the right asset categories and adopting effective entry and exit strategies.

Property Acquisition and Management

Real estate offers numerous wealth-building opportunities due to its lower risks and higher rates of return compared to other asset classes. Here are some key considerations for acquiring and managing properties:

1. **Property Acquisition:**
   - **Productive Farmland and Facilities:** Acquiring productive farmland or profitable production facilities.
   - **Multifamily Properties:** Investing in multifamily properties, such as apartment complexes, can be particularly lucrative.
   - **Valuation and Financing:** Understanding property valuation, financing options, and selection criteria.

2. **Management:**
   - **Income and Expenses:** Monitoring income and expense items to maximize property value.
   - **Market Trends:** Staying informed about market and economic changes to adjust rental prices effectively.
   - **Debt Service Coverage Ratio (DSCR):** Ensuring sufficient cash flow to cover debt obligations.

- **Net Operating Income (NOI):** Calculating NOI to determine property profitability.
- **Location and Accessibility:** Choosing properties in desirable locations with good accessibility.
- **Neighborhood Characteristics:** Assessing neighborhood quality and amenities.
- **Tenant Relationships:** Building positive relationships with tenants to ensure occupancy and rental income.

Real estate investors can adopt different approaches, whether as land and housing investors focusing on property appreciation or as business entrepreneurs generating rental income from multi-family units. Each strategy requires careful consideration of various factors, including property management, marketing, and legal aspects.

By understanding these principles and strategies, you can make informed decisions that enhance your real estate investment's profitability and long-term success.

5

Entrepreneurship and Business Ownership

Entrepreneurship and business ownership are powerful tools that many millionaires use to build their fortunes. By turning innovative ideas into successful ventures, they develop streams of passive income and amass significant wealth. German philosopher Arthur Schopenhauer once noted that the ability to start a business from scratch is a rare talent, one that many entrepreneurs possess.

Starting a new business is not as simple as flipping a switch; it often requires burning the midnight oil. The myth of the workaholic entrepreneur can be misleading, as successful business owners also know when to step back and diversify their investments. Some wealthy entrepreneurs have transitioned their businesses to family members, evolving their ventures into multi-million-dollar enterprises. Many entrepreneurs in our study have invested in small franchises, retaining their businesses while also investing profits in equities, bonds, or real estate. Although not all businesses sell for millions, selling a business can be a crucial step toward financial self-determination.

Starting and Scaling a Successful Business

Starting a business is a dream for many, with nearly 30 million small businesses in the United States alone. Here are some essential considerations for starting and scaling a successful business:

1. **Planning and Market Analysis:**
   - Perform thorough market analysis and planning.
   - Introduce yourself to community partners such as lenders, brokers, and accountants for additional wisdom and support.

2. **Strategic Growth:**
   - Consider key aspects such as current and anticipated employees, market demand, demographics, psychographics, and expenses.
   - Evaluate different growth strategies carefully, as scaling a small or mid-sized business can be risky.

3. **Transitioning Ownership:**
   - Key considerations include selling with or without a broker, understanding tax consequences, and planning for retirement.
   - Determine the value of your business through various valuation methods.

4. **Operational and Planning Considerations:**
   - Identify key players and their responsibilities within the enterprise.
   - Assess strengths, weaknesses, opportunities, and threats to your business concept and operations.
   - Remember that not every plan suits every person or locale.

For additional guidance, consider consulting with a Business Development Consultant who can help you determine the best course of action.

6

Risk Management and Insurance

Building wealth can be a slow process, but losing it can happen quickly, often due to unforeseen financial calamities. Planning for the future, including potential financial losses, is crucial. This section focuses on risk management, specifically through insurance, which is one of the most effective tools for minimizing risk exposure and providing a financial safety net.

Insurance products come in various forms, but at their core, they transfer the risk of loss to a larger pool of people. Here are some common types of insurance products:

- **Life Insurance:** Provides financial protection to your loved ones in the event of your death.
- **Auto Insurance:** Covers damages and liabilities related to car accidents.
- **Health Insurance:** Helps cover medical expenses.
- **Homeowner's Insurance:** Protects against damages to your home and personal property.

- **Renter's Insurance:** Covers personal property within a rental property.

Insurance companies also offer other services, such as investment vehicles and annuities, which provide returns or retirement income.

Why People Buy Insurance

People purchase insurance for various intangible reasons, such as peace of mind and the protection of loved ones, property, and wealth. Insurance protects against financial disaster, whether it's a car accident, a house fire, or a hospital stay. If insurance fulfills its purpose, the insured can retain their earnings while avoiding significant financial loss.

Managing Financial Risk

Managing the risks that lead to insurance payouts is a central concern for both insurers and policyholders. Nobody enjoys paying insurance premiums, but everyone wants the security insurance provides. Here are some common ways to mitigate financial risk:

1. **Life Insurance:**
   - **Advantages:** Provides financial security for beneficiaries.
   - **Disadvantages:** Premiums can be expensive, and policies can be complex.
   - **Mechanics:** Policyholders pay premiums, and beneficiaries receive a payout upon the policyholder's death.
2. **Auto Insurance:**
   - **Advantages:** Covers damages and liabilities related to car accidents.

- **Disadvantages:** Premiums vary based on driving history and vehicle type.
- **Mechanics:** Policyholders pay premiums, and the insurance company covers accident-related costs.

3. **Health Insurance:**
   - **Advantages:** Helps cover medical expenses.
   - **Disadvantages:** Premiums and out-of-pocket costs can be high.
   - **Mechanics:** Policyholders pay premiums, and the insurance company helps cover medical costs.

4. **Homeowner's and Renter's Insurance:**
   - **Advantages:** Protects against damages to property and personal belongings.
   - **Disadvantages:** Premiums vary based on property value and location.
   - **Mechanics:** Policyholders pay premiums, and the insurance company covers repair or replacement costs.

5. **Investment Vehicles and Annuities:**
   - **Advantages:** Provide returns or retirement income.
   - **Disadvantages:** Returns are not guaranteed, and fees can be high.
   - **Mechanics:** Policyholders invest premiums, and the insurance company provides returns or payouts over time.

By understanding these insurance products and their mechanics, individuals can better protect the wealth they've worked hard to build. Taking steps to mitigate financial risk is essential for long-term financial security and peace of mind.

7

Tax Planning and Wealth Preservation

Sound financial advice primarily focuses on retirement planning, guiding investment contributions, and asset allocation to reduce the amount necessary to accumulate for retirement. Once the foundation for retirement is established, other facets of wealth accumulation come into play, such as effective tax planning, asset protection, wealth distribution, and the creation of a special tax-free and guaranteed managed fund held by the family.

Effective wealth preservation involves several critical components:

1. **Minimizing Taxes:** Transferring assets to your family with minimal tax implications.
2. **Enhancing Net Income:** Increasing income while adhering to traditional tax laws and rates.

Tax Planning Techniques

Just as the IRS allows deductions for certain expenses incurred while generating income, it also recognizes the importance of life insurance. Life insurance is one of the most critical tools for wealth preservation and tax planning, available to everyone under current tax laws. Here's how it works:

- **Life Insurance:** Provides financial security and absorbs income in premium accumulation, allowing for significant tax advantages.
- **Efficient Tax Planning:** Techniques that trigger tax deductions and reduce estate tax liabilities, preserving the estate's principal for future generations.
- **Wealth Distribution:** Proper planning ensures that assets are passed to the next generation efficiently, minimizing tax burdens.

Wealth Preservation Strategies

Tax planning not only reduces obligations for money you don't spend during your lifetime but also minimizes taxes on the income and interest from your retirement distribution. Wealth preservation involves using insurance planning techniques, allowing insurance companies to leverage resources to your family's benefit. Here are some key strategies:

- **Insurance Planning:** Utilizing life insurance and other products to provide financial security and leverage.
- **Synchronizing Events:** Coordinating various financial events to achieve wealth preservation goals.
- **Guaranteed Managed Funds:** Establishing tax-free, family-managed funds for long-term wealth preservation.

By understanding and implementing these strategies, individuals can protect the wealth they have worked hard to build, ensuring financial security for themselves and their families.

8

Estate Planning and Legacy Building

While successful financial planning and investing are crucial aspects of building wealth, equally important is the structuring and preservation of your wealth for future generations. Estate planning and legacy building ensure that your hard-earned assets are efficiently transferred and protected after your passing. Though it may be difficult to contemplate our own mortality, addressing this issue is essential.

Fortunately, there are numerous tools and strategies provided by government bodies and financial institutions to aid in this endeavor. Here are some key components:

Estate Planning Considerations:

- **Wills:** Legal documents that outline your wishes for the distribution of your assets.
- **Heirs:** Individuals who will inherit your assets.
- **Inheritance:** The process of transferring assets to heirs.

- **Power of Attorney:** Legal authority for someone to act on your behalf.
- **Health Care Documents:** Directives that detail your medical care preferences.

Estate Planning Tools:

- **Percentage Bequests:** Allocating a percentage of your estate to beneficiaries.
- **Personal Property/Keepsakes:** Distributing cherished items to loved ones.
- **Spouse, Family, and Children:** Ensuring provision for your immediate family.
- **Favorite Christian Ministries:** Supporting charitable causes close to your heart.

Wealth Transfer Strategies:

- **Gifting Money to Family and Friends:** Reducing the taxable estate by giving gifts during your lifetime.
- **Family LLC:** A family limited liability company used for estate planning.
- **Charitable Remainder Trusts:** Trusts that provide income to you or your beneficiaries and a remainder to charity.
- **Dynastic Trusts:** Trusts designed to preserve wealth across multiple generations.
- **Gifting Stock to Children:** Transferring stocks as a form of inheritance.
- **Premium Financing of Life Insurance:** Using loans to pay for life insurance premiums.

Legacy Building:

- **Family Legacy:** Building and preserving a legacy that reflects your values and accomplishments.
- **Legacy Statement:** A document that articulates your vision and values for future generations.

The final section, **Legacy Building: What's Left?**, focuses on succession planning for your business, ensuring that your wealth continues to grow and support your family and causes you care about even after retirement. Estate and legacy building are about more than just preserving wealth; they are about making a lasting impact and providing for those closest to you.

By addressing these aspects, you can ensure a smooth transfer of wealth and provision for your loved ones, safeguarding the legacy you have worked hard to build.

9

Personal Development and Success Mindset

Behavioral and psychological attributes play a significant role in both creating and maintaining wealth. Self-dependence is crucial, and self-employed individuals are four times more likely to become millionaires than those who work for others. The prospects of better opportunities drive people to become more educated and self-sufficient.

The Importance of Self-Reliance and Risk-Taking

People who are willing to take risks and invest their resources into new or existing businesses are 3.4 times more likely to be wealthy than those who don't. They are also more likely to accumulate capital in certain businesses. Decisiveness and self-reliance are key traits consistently found among wealthy individuals.

The Success Mindset

A significant percentage (86%) of wealthy individuals are enthusiastic and focused on success. They have a strong belief in personal growth and take an active interest in current events and future-oriented activities. They also expand their social networks by participating in companies and local groups.

Developing a Success-Oriented Way of Thinking

Experts suggest that prospective millionaires should develop a success-oriented mindset. This includes:

- **Positive Affirmations:** Reinforcing positive thoughts and beliefs.
- **Power-Thinking:** Embracing powerful and optimistic thought processes.
- **Unorthodox Success:** Being open to unconventional paths to success.
- **Aspect Reframing:** Viewing challenges as opportunities.
- **Using Mentors:** Seeking guidance from successful individuals.

Continuous Personal Growth

The key to achieving success is continuous personal growth. Wealth is not just a result of financial strategies but also personalized knowledge, values, networks, and self-belief. Young, ambitious individuals often cite a lack of money as their primary obstacle, but the true challenge lies in who they must become to attract wealth.

By focusing on personal development and cultivating a success mindset, individuals can position themselves to achieve and sustain financial success.